IT WAS THERE
ALL ALONG

How I found happiness within everyday quotes

Rodrigo de la Maza de Teresa

ISBN-13: 9781234567890
ISBN-10: 9798590300594
ISBN: 9798590300594

Cover design by: Canvas
Library of Congress Control Number: 2018675309
Printed in the United States of America

To Lau
My Mom
My Brohers

PREFACE

> "Quit saying you don't have time. You have time
> for what you make time for in life."
> Bryant McGill

I've wanted to write a book about my thoughts for many years.
I had a lot of ideas and notes written down, but had not developed them into something that someone could read.
Then came 2020. Yes, Coronavirus.
Regardless of what you believe and think about it, it made me realize that I may not be able to write this tomorrow. Such is the fragility of life, but we usually don't understand it until it's as near to us as it is now.
So, with no time to spare, I set to put down most of what I've learned and how, all of which has helped me to be quite happy and at peace.
In the haste to get it done, I may have made some mistakes, omissions or grammatical errors. Please excuse me for those, for the purpose is greater than the form.

INTRODUCTION

"Whenever you find yourself on the side of the majority,
it's time to pause and reflect"
Mark Twain

Although I was always an inquisitive kid, curious, through my youth I mostly conformed to society's rules and ideas.
I went to school, obeyed my parents (most of the time) and played with my brothers, friends and neighbors.
A happy childhood I must admit, to which I credit having the time and freedom to think about some complex ideas for my age, as was the concept of God, infinity, eternity and other topics that other kids did not care about.
I kept thinking and questioning through my teens and into my twenties. Still I went to college, met the love of my life, married her and started our own family by the time I was 27. All in accordance to society's order.
It wasn't until we had been married for a few years that things started taking a different way.
We had the opportunity to travel and see bits of the world.
We had just bought an apartment and of course, being short on funds, did not have the resources to furnish it all.
Every time we saved enough to buy a dining room we would say: Should we buy the dining room or take a trip? The trip always won.
This meant that we had temporary furniture for a very long time.
Then came the first big controversial decision of our lives: Kids.

When we first got married, children were always in the picture. We even got the apartment with room for them and left one bedroom specially destined to our first.

Then, as the years went by and we travelled and enjoyed our lives, we started putting it off.

One day, on a trip (so fitting), driving along the M1 form London to Nottingham, the subject came up: Are we having kids or not?

We talked about it and very quickly thought about this: Having kids changes your life. We never questioned if it would be for the better or for worse, but were convinced it changed it.

So we asked ourselves: Do we want to change our lives?

And the answer was a resounding NO. We were happy, we loved traveling, our half furnished apartment had everything we needed, we had a company and job that we loved so NO, we weren't eager to change that.

So for now, we would not have kids. We were ok with everything and were not keen on any drastic changes.

One very important condition we agreed on: If one of us, at any point in time, wanted to have kids, the other one would cede, no questions asked. This removed the pressure for both of us if we ever changed our minds. And it worked wonderfully.

Society's pressure soon started. Our parents, brothers and sisters, uncles an aunts and even my grandmother insisted they wanted to see what our offspring would be like and have a new member in the family.

This went from subtle suggestion to open outrage by friends, some of which we lost in the process.

We soldiered on, got through the criticism and pressure and suddenly found ourselves feeling free and happy.

Note: I don't want to imply that not having kids makes you happy. It was just right for us. I'm sure many parents are very happy with their own decisions and live happy and fulfilling lives.

We kept travelling and I started running. My wife soon followed suit. We ran, travelled for marathons, trained for whatever we wanted and had time to eat out, work, read, vacation and gener-

ally enjoy and appreciate the life we were building for ourselves.
So this decision was a game changer. How could we have this positive effect from ONE decision away from convention?
Were we missing out on more abiding by the usual norms?
This started what I call my wake up period. The time that I started thinking more deeply about life, happiness and how the world generally steered us in a direction that may not be optimal for everyone.
I started observing situations in a new light and coming to my very own conclusions, which I later found, were rarely new to human kind.
Many ideas that I had were there many years before me, and most had been discussed at length.
However, the simple fact that they were conclusions at which I had arrived by myself, made them more valid to me and finding out I was not alone simply reinforced them.
I even started to find these ideas in popular quotes, many of which I had read or heard for years, but it was only at the relevant time that I understood their meaning.
So I went into the search of all of life's lessons and meaning in quotes from all ages and this led me to write this book.
Here I share with you some of the topics I've though about and the experiences and trains of though that led me to them, linking each to quotes that are not mine.
When I found the correct author of the quotes, I've included the credit.
The range of ideas goes from everyday realizations, to some deep and personal thoughts about our existence and the nature of the universe.
My only hope is to inspire and help you, dear reader, to reflect and come to your very own set of life beliefs, that help in your every day to make the most of the wonderful time we have this planet.
Most of the ideas are exposed in a single page.
Feel free to read the chapters in any order you like.

CHAPTER I

*"My life has been full of terrible misfortunes.
Most of which, never happened."*

Michel de Montaigne

When I was a boy I suffered from asthma.

I did not have it every day, it just happened to manifest on vacations.

As we vacationed a lot in an old family property, we all thought it might be an allergic reaction to the mold or dust from the walls or old ceilings.

For many years I managed to ruin my family's vacations with multiple visits to the emergency room in order to get penicillin shots and alleviate my symptoms somehow.

Both my mom and my dad worried a lot watching me grasp for breath and frankly to me, it felt horrible.

I visited many doctors and got pills and inhalers to control it. I even tried homeopathy.

However, it was on one particular trip to Acapulco that things changed.

I was 14 years old and just arriving for an amazing vacation on one of Mexico's most beautiful places, the Princess hotel in Acapulco.

A few hours after arriving, I started feeling the lack of air in my lungs and told my parents.

But wait. This was not that old family property. Walls and ceilings were perfectly clean and fine.

The air could not be fresher than that sea breeze.

My father sat me down and told me that from the doctors we had visited, he had learned that 50% asthma in all patients was psychological.

What?

I immediately understood that part of what was happening, was provoked by me.

Really? I was suffocating for no good reason?

I decided that at least that 50%, I was not going to contribute to.

There were some physical elements, but I was not going to amplify them with my stress, ideas or anxiety.

Almost immediately, my symptoms subsided and we ended up having a very nice family vacation.

From that day on, asthma was no longer an issue.

I don't know if I was crying for attention or subconsciously finding ways to punish my parents for something, but I was not having any of that anymore.

I was not going to create drama or illness in my head.

Many things in my life have since appeared where there is nothing. I simply let them by.

I do not succumb to the construction of thoughts of things that have not happened.

It's not only helped me live healthier and happier, bit also to be in the present and appreciate the now.

CHAPTER II

"*What we see depends mainly on what we look for.*"

John Lubbock

The top Mexican marketing and advertising magazine, Merca2.0 asked me to write a column about perception. No specific angle, open to submissions.

So I wrote about something that had happened to me recently.

I had just started to search for a house or apartment to buy and was very excited.

My wife and I went for many long street sweeping drives in the zones we wanted, to look for "For Sale" signs.

It turns out there were a lot.

And I mean a lot.

These were streets that we frequently drove through and it seemed that from one moment to the next, everything was for sale.

We talked about how funny this was and kept on looking.

A few weeks later I was looking at real estate signs everywhere, and to me, it seemed the whole city was full of them.

What happened? Had everything gone up for sale overnight?

And then I realized that no, that was not the case. Those signs had been there for some time now. Some of them even showed wear and tear from the weather.

So what was different?

I was looking for them.

I had been passing many of these streets every day and never no-ticed one but the day I started to look for them, they appeared.

You see? Things appear when you start opening up your mind to look for them.

I can only imagine what I would be able to see if I opened my mind and really absorbed everything that is before me. I'm working on that.

For now, I've learned that I see what I want to see.

CHAPTER III

"Comparison is the thief of Joy."

Theodore Roosevelt

In the first years of my professional life, I had to visit clients, suppliers and colleagues all over Mexico City. I had just bough a brand new Chevrolet Chevy. It was the smallest car in the country and the cheapest. Of course I still had to take out a loan to buy it.

Obviously it had no power windows or air conditioning, and it was a manual transmission, but it got me around and I was happy with it.

One day I was in heavy traffic. Tired of the clutch and the gear stick. It was very hot and I had my windows down, I was sweating and cursed my life and the car it provided me.

Besides me was a brand new BMW in which I was sure there was a person with very cool air conditioning, automatic transmission and a smoother overall ride, I was sure.

I envied him.

Then I saw a public transport van filled with people. Of course these vans did not have A/C either and I imagined the temperature in there with all those people.

I kept watching and found one person, leaning against the window with headphones on, happily bobbing her head to the rhythm of the music. She was smiling.

I realized, how could I complain about my situation? I was driving in my car, alone, with my own music headed for home to see my wife.

What had I to complain about?

That person gave me a lesson in humility and gratefulness. I was grateful of what I had, how my life was and made me reflect of things that I complained about.

I've complained a lot less since. Being grateful had turned what I had, into enough.

CHAPTER IV

"Expectation is the root of all heartache."

William Shakespeare

I have come to realize over time that many of life's frustrations come from waiting for something, from having expectations. Waiting for a response, waiting for an action, waiting for people to be grateful, waiting for reciprocity, in short, expecting something from people or the world.

Also reflecting on that, I realized that if you do things and only act to get a response or something from someone, you are probably doing it for the wrong reason.

So I concluded two things, which help a lot. You have to put them into practice:

1. Do things without expecting anything in return. It is the purest way of giving, living and doing something for others, for you and for the world.

2. Don't expect anything. If you don't expect anything, you will never get frustrated. And also, if something comes back, it will always be a pleasant surprise and you will appreciate it as such.

CHAPTER V

*"What you link pain to and what you link pleasure
to, shapes your destiny"*

Tony Robbins

A few years ago I came across the work of Tony Robbins, an American motivator who has helped thousands of people, on a massive scale, change their lives.

Beyond his method, which is interesting, he has concepts that I found excellent.

One of them stuck with me: Everything we do in life is to obtain pleasure, avoid pain, or a combination of the two.

Hearing it the first time, I instinctively thought it couldn't be. However, the more I digested it, I realized that it was true.

Think about it for a moment. You approach and provoke situations that give you pleasure and you move away and avoid what causes you pain.

So each act is linked to what each one has defined as pleasure and pain.

Now the interesting thing is that each of us has different definitions. Something that gives me pleasure may cause pain to someone else.

That means that to a certain extent, we have programmed ourselves to the things or situations that generate pleasure and pain for us.

The wonderful thing is that there is the possibility of changing the definitions for pain and pleasure for you. Tony has a pretty effective method of doing this. I recommend his works if you want to try it.

For me, the simple realization helped me be more at peace with my decisions.

CHAPTER VI

"Gratitude turns what we have into enough."

Aesop

Wealth doesn't come in the future, we already have it today. Being grateful for what we have and enjoying it is the best form of wealth.

This is not to say that we cannot have ambitions, but the way we think about them must be different. I read a phrase by Jim Rohn that said: "Be content with what you have, while pursuing what you want."

So longing or wanting something takes on a different perspective. There is no frustration for not achieving it and there is a great appreciation for having the possibility of pursuing and eventually achieving it.

The day I realized that I didn't need things to be happy, that continuing to compare other people's with mine would never lead to anything, that day I began to appreciate my life more and to live it with more intensity.

Also that day I realized that I had to think the same about myself. Be grateful for what I am and love myself that way. Great lessons come from small thoughts.

I'm already wealthy.

CHAPTER VII

"I only know that I know nothing"

Socrates

I've always been fascinated by learning and consider myself eclectic, since there are a myriad of topics that I like, from history to quantum physics.

Every time I stumble upon a new subject that peaks my interest, I dig into it in depth.

This had a boost when I read "The Da Vinci Code" by Dan Brown. I loved the story and the topic and though it was phenomenally well researched.

I set out to dig deeper in the subject and read almost every book mentioned in the novel like: "The Holy Blood and The Holy Grail" by Michael Baigent, Richard Leigh and Henry Lincoln and The Gnostic Gospels by Elaine Pagels.

This led me to read further into particular subjects like "James the Brother of Jesus" by Robert Eisenman.

After a few months I realized how much I didn't know about each of the subjects, and every time I read one book it sparked new curiosities. It led to many a rabbit hole.

After having satisfied my thirst for those subjects I started reading about mountain climbing, since it was something I was starting to do. Again, I read everything I could get my hands into.

I had until then considered myself an educated person. I did pretty well at the game Trivial Pursuit and the TV show Jeopardy. I always wanted to be the best informed in the room.

However the lesson for me was that I really knew very little and that there was a world of knowledge out there, which I would never be able to ingest.

This, instead of creating anxiety, gave me humbleness.

And this humbleness has made me open to hear anyone's opinion about anything and look at all the information that comes my way in a different light.

After all, I can learn a thing or two from it.

CHAPTER VIII

Everything that is going to happen to you in life is absolutely inevitable. There is nothing you can change.

Think about it for a minute. It is not a matter of destiny or determinism and it's not a philosophical question.

It is a premise as simple as saying "what will happen will happen and what will not, will not happen". It sounds even silly, but behind it I found an important learning.

As everything that is going to happen is going to happen and there is no way to avoid it, the only thing you can do about it is accept it, learn from it and take what you can.

With this I am not saying that you have to take a passive attitude towards life and wait for whatever comes, because I have always believed that each one builds their reality, but once things happen there is nothing that can be done about it.

This has given me peace, humility and challenged me to find the lessons, sometimes hidden, in every situation.

CHAPTER IX

*"The man who does not value himself, cannot
value anything or anyone."*

Ayn Rand

I was at a stop light in Mexico City when I had this thought.

Waiting for the green light, a lady comes over to the window of my car asking for spare change. I gave her some money and felt good. Like I had done a good deed not wanting anything in return.

I went on my way.

Thinking about it later, that good feeling of having helped, in a small way, another human being I reflected that I was getting something in return for my kindness. I was feeling good with myself.

Was what I did really a selfless act? No, I reflected. I did it because it would make me feel good too.

I started thinking about other things that I did selflessly in my life like helping an employee, opening the door for my wife, giving someone a gift. Everything provided me with a clear benefit, feeling good.

In the end, everything I did benefited me in one way or another, so I realized I was actually being selfish!

I am selfish. Proudly.

Being selfish doesn't mean you have to be a bad person and the concept is very well explained by Ayn Rand in "The Virtue of Selfishness".

It just means accepting that everything we do is for our own benefit. Do not be fooled otherwise.

Think about it, even giving your life for another person is not selfless. It's a way to avoid living with yourself if you had not done it.

I asked all my Facebook friends to give me one example of a selfless act, and after several attempts, they all accepted they did everything to feel good themselves in one way or another.

I put this test to you now. Think of one selfless thing or act that you consider so and reflect how it benefited you.

I propose that we accept ourselves as we are and keep on living the same way with one difference: The conscious thought that everyone is looking out for themselves, as you are.

CHAPTER X

"I am not a product of my circumstances. I am a product of my decisions."

Stephen Covey

I have come across all kinds of people in my life and have realized that there are only two types: 1. The victims, to whom everything happens, the world conspires against them, they have bad luck and they constantly blame to others for everything and 2. People who understand that they build their own reality and their life, that they are participants in what happens to them.

It is very easy to locate a victim. If he is late it's the fault of traffic, if he does not have a job it's because no one appreciates his talent, he constantly complains about others and the government is responsible for everything.

It is also easy to spot someone who is responsible for her life. She knows that there are things that she cannot change and she accepts them, she learns from them. In everything else, where she can influence, she acts. She acts in the direction in which she expects the response of what she does. She is a positive person, with an energy that stops at nothing

I read a sentence that helped me complete this part of my personal philosophy: You cannot change what happens, but you can change how you take it.

So I choose to take things in a positive way, being optimistic and trying to learn from everything that happens.

CHAPTER XI

"When someone else's happiness is your happiness, that is love."

Lana del Rey

When I was a boy, I always thought about what I would ask for to the genie in Aladdin's lamp.

Back then, the cold war was at its peak, so somehow I was thinking how we could all live in peace. Each had their point of view, their goals, and their fears and there was no way I could know all of them.

I thought: "Well, if I feel at peace that's enough", but then I thought, what if my parents and my brothers were not at peace? What was needed then for them to be at peace too?

It got complicated. And I was 10 years old.

Until finally I thought that I only needed one wish and that that would be enough: I want everyone to be happy.

I know, it is not an easy task, but I understood in my mind that everyone has their own version of what makes them happy and if everyone got what they wanted, whatever it was, we could live in a world where we would all be happy and there would be no war.

Simplistic perhaps, but that was one of the first philosophical thoughts I had on my own.

CHAPTER XII

"Beware the tyranny of routine"

Gordon Toy

Do you ever feel that a year has gone bye and it has all happened so fast? And in contrast, do you remember how, as a little kid, a year was an eternity?

I happened to go to a restaurant frequently. It was close to my house, the food was good and the staff very friendly.

Although there was a large menu, I often ordered the same two or three dishes. This went on for years.

On one occasion there was a special plate with seasonal ingredients. I wanted to try it and it was delicious. I remember that lunch very vividly. I had a nice time, a good talk and an especially fine meal.

Why am I telling you this? Because I can't remember much specific from any of the other lunches at that restaurant. They were pretty much replicated experiences.

But that particular day, with that different dish, I remember well.

The perception of the passage of time, that it accelerates, has to do with not experiencing new things, which enrich your mind, body or spirit. As we grow, more things are known, common and so they happen quickly.

This is specially experienced with our customs and everyday

routines. When you do the same things over and over, you stop distinguishing one experience from another.

Take a different street to work.

Walk instead of taking the car.

Try something new at that restaurant.

You'll remember those experiences better and the perception of the passage of time will slow down and allow you to experience more of life.

CHAPTER XIII

"Everyone you meet is fighting a battle you know nothing about. Be kind. Always."

Brad Meltzer

When I was 21 I opened my first company, an advertising agency, with my two best friends. Very soon my wife joined and we worked very hard to get clients and make a name for ourselves.

As we grew and things started to be more complex I started having differences with one of my friends, now my partner as well.

We had different visions of how to compensate ourselves. I was in a happy relationship, looking to get married and rent an apartment.

This required more resources, so I needed more money. The company had it, but my partner did not want to take more money out. He wanted to get more profits at the end of the year.

Of course, he lived with his father and had no girlfriend, so he needed very little money to get by.

This grew to be such a huge discussion that we ended up splitting up, and I had to buy his share of the company.

At the time I was very mad at him and could not believe he didn't understand my position. He was going to have more money anyway, for his higher salary.

I carried a grudge and I did not like it.

One day, as I was running, I reflected on the subject. I knew this guy very well for several years. I stepped into his shoes and realized that he had been true to his beliefs and thoughts. He had no option but to think as he has and I finally understood that. If I had been in his shoes, I would have done exactly the same thing. Knowing him, his education, his beliefs, his intelligence, I knew he could not have acted any differently.

At this exact moment I realized I could not judge him for what he had done and decided.

Also I could not judge myself. I had done what I could do with the tools I had and under those circumstances.

A huge weight lifted from my shoulders.

Everyone does the things they do because they have no choice. That is how they think, that is the information they have and that's how they feel about it. That can't be changed.

I realized I could not judge anyone for anything ever again, because I certainly did not know everything that person thought and felt.

Also, I realized I could stop judging myself as well. Everything I did in the past has it's own moment, reason and perfect explanation, at the time.

Every decision I have made was the best I could have made. Of course as you learn and mature, you might look at things differently, but it's not fair to judge your past based on the person you are now.

We are evolving and growing beings and every day makes us different from the last.

So don't be so hard on yourself. Accept your decisions and be grateful for them, because of them, you are who you are today.

This has helped me be at peace with myself and with others.

CHAPTER XIV

Galileo Galilei

Through the yeas I've realized that we are all experiencing life at a different rate and from different points of view.

This means that we are all learning and maturing different stuff at different times.

I always wondered why when sharing my thoughts and experiences with someone, they seemed to not listen and go about their same way, provoking suffering from themselves that I thought they could have avoided.

It's not that I was the bearer of the truth or correct way to do things. It's just that sharing experiences was my way of trying to help people avoid some of the mistakes I'd made and the hardships that came from them.

Then I read a phrase that resounded with this: "When the student is ready, the teacher appears" by Lao Tzu.

That means that we are not all ready at the same time to learn something, it's like trying to teach calculus to a 5 year old when he is barely understanding arithmetic.

And you cannot force the process.

I've stopped trying to teach anyone anything. I am no one to do so.

I can only live by my beliefs and principles, hoping that I contribute something to someone.

CHAPTER XV

I've been a runner for many years, even dabbling in triathlons and mountain climbing.

When I ran my first 10k I was hooked. I wanted more. The experience of the race itself was exhilarating but the idea that I had trained and that training resulted in me completing it, was addictive.

I started training more and entering longer races. 15k, half marathon, marathon, another marathon, you get the picture.

Soon running and marathons seemed to be limiting me, so I entered an ultra marathon, then triathlons and up to an Ironman Race.

After that I switched to trail races with huge elevation gains and that brought me to mountaineering, after one particular race on a volcano in Mexico.

When I reached the top the view was so beautiful that I decided I wanted more of that.

So, I started to climb, first Mexico's volcanoes and then Mt. Rainier in the US.

A friend of mine casually shared that he wanted to climb Mt. Everest. At the time I thought he was crazy but after my years and athletic achievements, the idea lingered in my mind.

I began planning the path to Everest. Read every book available about the subject. Learned about the mountains I could climb in preparation and even thought of ways to be sponsored. I was on my way.

After a brief hiatus, I went over my plan and thought Everest is the hardest thing a man can do. Of course there are other mountains with other difficulties, but climbing Everest would be the pinnacle of my athletic life.

And then in dawned on me. What would I do after Everest? Would there be longer races? Could I climb it solo and without oxygen?

I realized I had been running and climbing in a rat race fashion, only to go further, faster and higher every time.

I had stopped enjoying every race and climb because I always had the next one in my sight.

Except, I thought, after Everest.

So if I did not start enjoying the training, the preparation, for itself, it would lead to a short lived feeling of accomplishment, followed by what?

It didn't matter, I realized I was running and climbing for the wrong reason. I was doing it to prove to myself I could do more. In the process I had missed the scenery, literally.

So I decided to forget about races and goals and started to do it all just for the enjoyment.

I still run and exercise regularly, but do it without a watch and without a specific goal.

I enjoy the trees, the sun, the woods and the fresh air.

Every workout is now a complete joy in itself.

CHAPTER XVI

*"I wish everyone could experience being rich and famous,
so they'd see it wasn't the answer to anything."*

Jim Carrey

When I was growing up, especially in high school and through college, money was scarce in my family.

We had enough to live simply, but there were no luxuries or trips of any kind for several years.

When I started working and earning money, I realized I could buy stuff and finally have the things that I had wanted.

I bought clothes, electronics, furniture, a bicycle and soon, almost anything I could want. Good thing I never wanted a yacht or a jet.

Any way, this went on for some time and I never lost the opportunity to get the latest running ware or shoes or to have a watering can sent from England for my Bonsai.

Up till that point I though happiness came from achieving what I wanted and being able to acquire whatever I decided.

Somehow a good income, a car, a house and lots of travel would make me happy.

Then, one day, while cleaning out my old running clothes in order to make room for new ones, I found a brand outfit at the bottom of the drawer. The labels were still on the items.

I realized that I had been buying clothes just for the sake of buying them, not because I needed them.

This moment, I realized I had everything I needed. I have had for a while.

I had been caught up in the rat race.

I was not getting any happier for buying and having stuff. Of course there was a little joy every time I took something new out of a shopping bag, but it did not amount to happiness.

Material stuff was not doing the job and also I realized that the race I was in, would never end.

There would always be a better car, a bigger house or a more extravagant trip to take.

I decided there and then to stop buying useless stuff and quit the race.

I actually went the opposite direction and started cleaning out stuff I didn't use, selling other that I no longer wanted and generally purging my life.

This has made my life simpler and more fulfilling.

I feel lighter and renewed, like I've made space in my life, and having space to spare is always good, you never know what may come.

CHAPTER XVII

"True love begins when nothing is looked for in return"

Antoine de Saint-Exupery

Real love is giving without expecting anything in return.

When you expect something in return you are giving your love with conditions. This means that if you are not reciprocated in some way, you get frustrated, mad or sad.

On the other hand when you love and give the best of yourself, just for your own pleasure and satisfaction, anything that comes back, if it does, is a pleasant surprise.

I've found that this realization gives me more freedom to love, in a purer manner.

Love unconditionally, you'll be happier.

CHAPTER XVIII

"Everyone thinks about you far less than you think they do."

Anonymous

After a few years of working, we had a healthy portfolio of clients and were growing constantly.

Then, one of my clients called me in for a meeting and told me that they would no longer be working with us. I asked why and he said that we were a small agency and that they wanted a bigger one, with award winning creative staff. This was the first time a client had fired us. And essentially, fired me.

Fortunately this was not a big client and we did not lose very much income. The very next day we landed a new client that made up for that loss and with a little more to spare, so the impact on the company, financially, was very small.

However, having lost our first client I was troubled. I was up at night thinking of how I could have prevented it and what I could do to avoid it in the future.

There were some lessons of course and we implemented a lot, which helped us be better.

However, I felt at odds. Even though the agency was doing well, clients were happy and the staff motivated.

I realized that what bothered me was my ego. I didn't want anyone to know that we had lost the client because I was afraid of what they would think of me. Would they see me as a looser? Was

I capable of running my own company?

All my insecurities surfaced.

After a few weeks I found that no one really cared so much as to devote their time and energy to think about me and my failures. I was not the center of everyone's thoughts.

This liberated me and at the same time taught me that I had been miserable the last few weeks only because of my ego.

Dam you ego.

I reflected on how much stuff in my life was being dictated by my ego and found out that it was a lot.

I decided to work on liberating me from my own ego. It turned out that I had the solution to my sleepless nights within me.

It's a tough battle and I still have to check myself from time to time, but am constantly improving and being happier and more at peace for it.

CHAPTER XIX

"This is your life and it's ending one minute at a time"

Tyler Durden

When I was a kid I started thinking about God, heaven and hell.

I was brought up loosely Catholic, but my Grandmother, whom I loved deeply, insisted on me learning about religion.

Frankly it bothered me in several fronts. Rationally I could not understand God's eternity. For one thing, he had been there forever and would be there forever. I could not grasp the concept. After all, there had to be something before, right?

On the other hand, the idea of hell and that if I wasn't good I would go there when I died, also stuck in my head.

I was not happy with something or someone passing judgment on the decisions in my life to have a say in weather I went to one place or the other.

So, I was at odds as to how to live my life.

And then it dawned on me, it doesn't matter if there is a God or not and if I believed he would judge me. I won't get into more detail on that subject here.

What I did think of is that I was not going to live my life worrying about what happened after.

I was certain of only one thing: I was here now.

That's all I actually had and have.

No guarantees on anything else.

So, not being a gambling man, I chose to focus my energy in getting the most out of every moment.

Whatever happens after is up for grabs and you may have your own predictions. I have mine.

I choose not to speculate and since it's ending one minute at a time, I'd better get on with living and making the most of the wonderful time I've been granted here.

CHAPTER XX

"The mind is everything. What you think you become."

Buddha

I've read many ideas about how your thoughts make the path of your life.

You probably know the way. What you think becomes what you say, and what you say becomes what you do, and all that determines who you are and what life you live.

But when I read Dr. Bruce Lipton's "The Biology of Belief", the subject took to a whole new level.

In his book he goes into the science behind what we think, and he bases his book on quantum physics and biology. Science.

Look up the double-slit experiment and how matter can be both a particle and a wave at the same time.

I'm not going to go too deeply into the subject but long story short, matter only takes into one form or the other when you observe it.

That's right, the simple fact of you observing something makes it take a form.

This concept baffled even Einstein back in his days, but it's one of the most accurately and broadly proven facts of today's physics.

What does this mean?

That you literally create your own reality. What you think of and what you say, and so on, literally make things happen in your life.

So for this one idea, please forgo the philosophical angle and trust the science.

What you think of, what you visualize, what you believe, all become your very own reality.

So be careful.

Be mindful.

This subject will change your life. For better or worse, so be conscious of what you want and think.

CHAPTER XXI

"Spend some time alone every day"

The Dalai Lama

Through the years I've become very comfortable with being alone. All by my self. Even though my immediate family is just my wife, our two dogs and me in our house, I do enjoy the time I have for myself.

I never get bored, lack things to do or entertain myself with.

However, the greatest benefit from this has been that I've had time to think about stuff.

Most people are so busy that the barely have time to get everything they have to do, done.

I'm busy as well, but make it a point to have some time for me every day.

This may be when I go out for a run, when walking the dog, or at night when everyone is asleep.

This time is precious to me and lets me reflect on any topic that I'm finding relevant at the time.

I find that I enjoy every day more, being alone with my thoughts.

I know more than one person who doesn't like to be alone. They are constantly seeing friends, making plans, and make it a point to have their lives full.

I don't know why they do it, and there may be many different reasons for it, but I am sure they haven't found the peace and joy of having only to deal with your own thoughts.

When you can comfortably be alone, you instantly become better company, because you don't need someone else to be happy, it simply becomes someone you can share it with, which is very nice, by the way.

CHAPTER XXII

"Karma means you have to live with the consequences of the actions you have taken in the past. Whatever you put out is coming back"

Deepak Chopra

I used to be an angry driver. As you may know, Mexico City is filled with cars and those with a lot of rude drivers.

So it was a guarantee that if I had to take my car somewhere, a driver would cut me off, someone would cut the line in an exit or any other of the usual rudeness that's common in a big city.

I used to get mad, honk the horn, even on occasion, shouting at the driver who had provoked the rage.

Then, one day I thought, the person that just cut me off will probably cut off a dozen more drivers, he will get shouted at, insulted and may end up in a street fight. At the end of his journey, he'll probably be in a foul mood and that's not a nice way to live.

So I decided that all those rude drivers were getting the punishment from their actions, all by themselves. Their life probably reflected that rudeness in their home or office or even within themselves. It's easy to get gastritis, an ulcer or high blood pressure if they have to go through that every day.

Anyway, I decided that I did not need to educate anyone, to point out their infractions or to make sure they suffered the consequences or their actions.

This is when I thought of Karma, and the idea that you pay for everything wrong that you do. It works both ways, for good and bad. You get what you give.

And this also resonated with me as a law of the universe, expressed in many ways. The universe has a way to achieve a balance.

So, the universe or Karma would take care of the revenge I sought and I started to trust this in everything in life.

This has made me a very cool and nice driver. I always let others pass, brake for pedestrians (I know it should be normal, but in Mexico City is not common) and enjoy my every drive a lot more.

Every time I receive any rudeness, I always think about that poor person and the problems he must face every day.

As an added benefit, I get genuine appreciation from drivers when letting them by and smiles from pedestrians that are not used to someone stopping to let them cross the street.

Of course this applies to everything and everyone, so I've applied it to all the aspects of my life.

This has lead to me not getting mad at all. My family and friends have asked me how can I not be mad about this or that. I always respond that life gives you back what you give it. I decide to be nice and when I don't receive niceness, I let it pass.

CHAPTER XXIII

"Be the architect of your future. Not a prisoner of your past."

Deepak Chaurasiya

When I was a boy, both my parents went to see a therapist. It was very nouvelle at the time and they openly discussed it.

I remember my mother telling me that this person would get her to remember things from her life or her past, that would explain her behavior and decisions today. Very Freudian.

This made me think that I was not only a product of my past, but later on, a prisoner of it.

I had my share of insecurities and anxieties as a teen and well into my twenties and tried to think and discover what, in my past, made me de like that.

I never got to the root of the problems.

As I grew and matured most of those issues disappeared and the others lost importance. The problems and the priorities changed.

I was still a shy person, some may even call me an introvert.

I was especially shy about asking for any favors. I was happy to do them for others but always tried to manage what I needed for myself. Pride was getting the best of me.

Many years later I started a project with my brother and an ex partner, which was very promising.

It involved advertising in outdoor media.

But in order to be successful I had to call up most of the people I knew and ask for their help.

You understand this challenged me in two ways: call them and ask for help.

I'd never done this before but I read the quote that titles this chapter and decided in an instant I did not have to be the shy man that solved everything himself, without help, anymore.

One decision was all it took. Nothing in my past held me down.

I called everyone I needed and to my surprise, everyone was eager to help and some even went the extra mile to push the project themselves.

My shyness and pride went out the door.

I knew that I could do the same with any other belief or limitation that I had.

Only because I'd had it for a long time it didn't mean I could not change it in a second.

So, don't let your past, or what you think of it, hold you back.

You can actually venture yourself to do anything you want by just deciding it. It really is that easy. Give it a try.

CHAPTER XXIV

"Everything happens for you, not to you."

Byron Katie

I had been a runner for a few years now and was training for the New York City Marathon.

I had sent my entry and fortunately got the spot. I wanted this to be my best marathon yet.

I set out to plan my training, planning to reduce my race time by at least 5 minutes.

The training was hard. Repetitions at high speed, intense tempo sessions and several long runs, increasing the mileage every week.

10 weeks away from the marathon, I got injured.

Something or other to do with my iIiotibial band made my knee hurt as hell and I had to stop.

I went to the orthopedist and he said I suffered from Iliotibial Band Syndrome. Taking my body too far too soon, resulted in swelling of the tissue.

There was nothing I could do except rest, go to therapy and take my medicine. My record setting marathon dreams were over.

I was really devastated. The trip was all paid for, the marathon entry had been hard to get and I didn't want to miss my chance.

So I did as directed and rested, took my pills but most annoyingly, went to therapy.

The therapy clinic was a good hour and fifteen minutes from my office. It took an hour to get done and then the same drive back. Four hours of every weekday dedicated to this.

Also, since I had a lot of work, I could not leave the office early, so I had to schedule the therapies at the latest time of day possible, which resulted in me being stuck in traffic all the time. On both the way over and back.

Needless to say these drives for the next six weeks were tough.

I had nothing to do on them but complain to myself, be miserable and curse my luck.

And then something wonderful happened.

I discovered audio books.

Audible.com was then, as now, the best option for audio books. Endless topics and authors.

So I started reading/listening to books in the car.

This changed the tone of therapy.

I couldn't wait to leave the office to listen to my book and guess what? I could listen while getting the therapy as well.

So I read an average of two books a week during those six weeks.

I was not in a mood for novels or business books, so I read a lot about philosophy, ideas and thinkers.

Some of those books are the ones that taught me about patience, humility, perseverance and generally, ideas and topics that inspired me to white this.

I finished my therapy, got to train a little more for the marathon and ran it.

Of course it wasn't my best time, but I was very happy and satisfied with having done it and in the process, discovered a new and wonderful way of learning new stuff.

So you see? My injury had a reason, a purpose.

I discovered and embraced it.

Now I understand that things happen. You can't change the circumstances.

But if you look carefully enough, you will see something good behind it and it's up to you to make the best of that situation, and learn in the process.

At the same time, frustration and anger fade away.

So, thank you iliotibial band, for letting up and making me stop only to discover something so enriching.

CHAPTER XXV

"Nothing ever goes away until it teaches us what we need to know."

Pena Chodron

When we first landed an account at the advertising agency, we were very happy. We finally had a client on retainer that provided us with some steady income month by month.

We carefully looked at our fixed costs, assigned ourselves a small part of it and started to operate with some cash flow.

However, we did need to hire an account executive for that client. That was a huge fixed cost for us but we believed in ourselves and accepted the amount as an investment in the future and growth of the company.

The next account would get us out of the hole.

It worked, kind of.

We got to land another client and more income came.

For this client, we had to buy expensive software for their media buy, again we invested practically the entire margin in doing this, because we were on a roll, and we would get new clients.

The next account would get us out of the hole.

And guess what? We were right. We did get a new client after that. This one required us to produce a lot of printed materials, so we had to hire someone specialized in the subject to help get it done. It was an investment.

The next account would get us out of the hole.

And then we landed the biggest client we had ever had. Fourfold.

This was a big fish that any agency in Mexico would want.

The thing was, that in order to get their business we had to hire their favorite creative director. He came with a hefty price tag.

We closed the deal.

The next account would get us out of the hole.

It then dawned on me. I had been thinking that the next account would get us out of the hole for many years.

Was the next account the solution to all our problems? It hadn't happened yet.

So I took a deep dive into our organization, the staff, our fixed costs and found a way to make things profitable with the accounts we had, not relying on the next to fix it.

Had I done this some years earlier, we would have been in a better financial situation.

I learned my lesson and from then on profits took a different and positive direction.

I had to have this problem over and over to understand that I had to do things differently in order to get out of it.

Remember this the next time you see an issue or problem appear frequently and repeatedly in your life.

It's probably there for a reason and if you give it a moment, reflect and try something different, you may stumble con the way to get rid of it for good.

CHAPTER XXVI

"If you want something you never had, you have
to do something you've never done"

Thomas Jefferson

My father was a person that loved food. He really enjoyed the flavors and textures of everything.

Food was such a huge part of his life that he devoted many hours a day to the topic. At home, selecting dishes and menus and when travelling he always had a restaurant for every meal previously selected and reserved.

I liked food too and enjoyed it but never really to his extent.

When I got married, my wife introduced me to new dishes and flavors. She loves to cook but found little joy in making anything too elaborate because it made little difference to me.

Eventually my diet became a string of the same combination of dishes: Some kind of fish, shrimp, rice and salad with basically the same two or three dressings. Occasionally a steak or hamburger but again, nothing too nouvelle.

Then, I became a vegan. From one day to the next I realized that I didn't liking what I was putting in my body and since I firmly believe you are what you eat, I stopped eating all animal products.

The problem was that I only eliminated the animal products and added nothing. For a few weeks I only ate the same salads and vegetables along with whole grain bread.

My wife started coming up with new dishes and re inventing others in a vegan version.

We started to visit vegan restaurants and discovered new flavors, preparations and options. Much of this was very new to us and a total deviation from the flavors and textures we were used to.

And then, 2020 happened. Lock down. Social distance. Stay at home.

So now in order to have a really good meal we'd have to prepare it at home.

And as you may imagine, diversity was part of the challenge.

I had never really cooked. You know, pasta, grill, the basics. The kitchen did not appeal to me very much.

But if I wanted to keep experimenting and finding new flavors, I would have to help and contribute preparing new things myself.

Within a couple of months and with the help of Youtube, I had learned to prepare vegan tuna for sandwiches, a vegan egg salad, vegan potato cheese, vegan nacho cheese, vegan smoked salmon, teppanyaki vegetables and yakimeshi rice.

I learned to make my own pizza dough and pie and have tried dozens of recipes with pizza dough (which I love!).

I even baked a vegan apple crumble which my wife says is one of the most delicious she's ever tried.

It turns out you can learn to cook and find your own flavors. So, for this, I thank you Coronavirus.

Thank you for helping me get out of my comfort zone and learning something new while discovering the richness of the plant based diet.

Imagine all you can discover when you step outside your comfort zone.

I'm looking forward to wandering outside mine a lot more.

CHAPTER XXVII

"Quiet the mind and the soul will speak."

Ma Jaya Sati Bhagavati

My Mom has always been a spiritual being and when I was a kid she lead meditation classes at our home.

I frequently joined and eventually learned about different topics, from meditating, to The Course of Miracles, to the fourth way, Tarot, Carlos Castaneda, and some parapsychology stuff that I will not go into detail now.

Anyway, I was introduced to a myriad of spiritual topics of which I understood only a fraction, but some stuff stuck with me.

I learned to meditate, really clear my mind and be present in the moment.

So many guided meditations and breathing exercises helped me incorporate meditation into my everyday life.

I don't have to sit down for a dedicated hour to do it daily, I've learned to meditate while driving, while doing chores and specially, while running.

Everyone talks about the runner's high and how when you get there, your body's in auto pilot, you are not thinking of anything and you get into a rhythm that you feel that can go on forever.

That state, that feeling, comes from clearing your mind, and being in the moment.

I've found that if I can make a few of this moments, as brief as the may be, in my every day life, I get the same soothing, calming, balancing feeling.

My head feels clearer, my feelings in check and ready to tackle whatever hurdle is next.

You are probably meditating already in some part of your life. Acknowledge it and keep it.

You're giving your soul a chance to speak.

CHAPTER XXVIII

"You can't calm the storm, so stop trying. What you can do is calm yourself. The storm will pass."

Timber Hawkeye

I have found that I can't control my feelings. Nor understand them.

Reading about the subject it turns out you can't understand your feelings because they happen in a different part of the brain.

I've also understood that for this same reason, feelings are provoked automatically as a primal reaction to something. So primal that many times that we don't understand where they come from.

Now, when you try to rationalize a feeling and start building stories around it, it becomes an emotion.

You start associating things that happen in your life to it, you start thinking what you did to provoke this and sometimes you even start provoking that feeling in your own mind by creating stories of things that have not happened.

This is when a feeling turns into an emotion and you are making the effects of that feeling bigger and prolong it within you. In this situation, you are letting an emotion rule you and your life.

I once read that we should think about feelings as a cloud in the sky. The cloud forms, takes a shape and eventually moves on.

When a feeling strikes, you can acknowledge it, give it space within you and watch it go.

It usually lasts only a couple of minutes if you just let it be.

This way, emotions will not rule you.

Thank Timber Hawkeye from Buddhist Boot camp for making this topic easily digestible.

CHAPTER XXIX

"One more thing"

Steve Jobs

Drink more water. Get yourself a glass and have it besides you always. I guarantee you drink it and will be happier and healthier for it.